Waters

Living

It Takes Two

FRANK SENNETT

It Takes Two

Wise Words and Quotable Quips
on the Attraction of Opposites

Contemporary Books

Chicago   New York   San Francisco   Lisbon   London   Madrid   Mexico City
Milan   New Delhi   San Juan   Seoul   Singapore   Sydney   Toronto

The McGraw·Hill Companies

Library of Congress Cataloging-in-Publication Data

Sennett, Frank.
   It takes two / Frank Sennett.
      p.   cm.
   ISBN 0-07-140559-3
   1. Quotations, English.   2. Wit and humor.   I. Title.

   PN6084.H8 .S46   2002
   081—dc21

2002023445

Copyright © 2003 by The McGraw-Hill Companies, Inc. All rights reserved. Printed in the United States of America. Except as permitted under the United States Copyright Act of 1976, no part of this publication may be reproduced or distributed in any form or by any means, or stored in a database or retrieval system, without the prior written permission of the publisher.

1 2 3 4 5 6 7 8 9 0   LBM/LBM   1 0 9 8 7 6 5 4 3 2

ISBN 0-07-140559-3

Interior design by Diane Jaroch

McGraw-Hill books are available at special quantity discounts to use as premiums and sales promotions, or for use in corporate training programs. For more information, please write to the Director of Special Sales, Professional Publishing, McGraw-Hill, Two Penn Plaza, New York, NY 10121-2298. Or contact your local bookstore.

This book is printed on acid-free paper.

This book is for Heather, who seems to love me no matter what type of person I am; and for Ted, who truly was one of a kind.

Contents

PREFACE ix

ACKNOWLEDGMENTS xv

OPPOSITE ATTRACTIONS 1

LOVE CONNECTIONS 27

FRIENDSHIPS AND FAMILY AFFAIRS 69

MARRIED TO THE JOB 85

EMBRACING OPPORTUNITY 105

WHINE AND DINE 117

ANIMAL INSTINCTS 125

FOR LOVE OF THE GAME 129

THE SHOPPING CALL 135

HOME SUITE HOME 143

DRIVING PURSUITS 149

Preface

There may be said to be two classes of people in the world: those who constantly divide the people of the world into two classes and those who do not.

In coining Benchley's Law of Distinction, legendary *New Yorker* humorist Robert Benchley took a wry swipe at the notion of sorting everyone into polar-opposite groups. Silly or not, the practice is more popular today than ever—especially when it comes to relationships and matters of the heart.

We kid our spouses and significant others about the sometimes endearing, sometimes annoying traits we find in each other. He channel surfs, while she sticks with one station all day. She balances her checkbook to the penny, while he keeps an extra hundred dollars in the bank to compensate for his fuzzy spending math. She can't get ready in time for an evening out, but if he's in charge they'll be the party's first awkward guests.

PREFACE

Tomato, tomahto. Potato, potahto. But we don't always call the whole thing off, do we? In fact, as they say, opposites do tend to attract. Maybe it's because differences in outlook and style keep things interesting.

From our teens on, we ponder the differences between puppy lovers and soul mates, fast-burning romances and long-smoldering passions, close-knit families and strained relations, fair-weather pals and friends for all seasons—encompassing all of our relationships, both cherished and crumbled.

There are two kinds of people in the world, and I am one of them.
—HUMORIST DAVE BARRY

Everywhere you turn in the popular culture, it seems, there are two kinds of people: Luke Skywalker or Han Solo. Betty or Veronica. Letterman or Leno. Lucy or Ethel. Goofus or Gallant. Barbie or G.I. Joe. Private school or public school. First class or coach. Paper or plastic. Two percent or skim. New or used.

Buy or lease. Cash or charge. Coastal residents or "flyover people." Less filling. Tastes great.

There can be an almost symbiotic relationship between groups that seem to be at odds. Would the adorable Beatles and the bad-boy Rolling Stones have enjoyed such phenomenal success throughout the 1960s without having each other to play against? Would fat funnymen Oliver Hardy and Lou Costello have been nearly as hysterical without their rail-thin straight men Stan Laurel and Bud Abbott?

Speaking of high comedy, haven't the Republicans and Democrats pulled off a neat trick by excluding third-party candidates to the unelectable fringes of the nation's political process? If you don't know the answer to that one, just ask Ralph Nader.

Maybe this "two kinds of people" stuff all goes back to our most distant ancestor, a single-celled organism that just had to split. Or maybe you're that other type of person, who sees

PREFACE

Adam and Eve atop the family tree of humanity. Luckily, there's room enough for both kinds of people, if we choose to respect each other's beliefs.

There are two kinds of people, those who finish what they start and so on.
—HUMORIST ROBERT BYRNE

When it comes to quote books like the one you're holding, there are definitely two kinds of people: those who dutifully read the preface, and those who skim it before diving headlong into the trove of collective wisdom that comes after. To both types of readers, welcome—and thanks.

In this book, you'll find humorous observations and keen cultural insights from a wide array of columnists, journalists, novelists, poets, playwrights, diarists, essayists, critics, and humorists—as well as an eclectic group of smart famous folk that includes U.S. presidents, senators, governors, foreign heads of state, actors, musicians, television and radio personalities, sports stars, business gurus, military leaders, religious thinkers, and even a pioneering astronaut.

Us and them. We and they. Me and you. It may not be scientifically accurate, this urge to divide the world into halves. But it sure is fun.

Acknowledgments

There are two kinds of people I wish to acknowledge and thank: those who so generously contributed to my professional development and those who provided inspiration with their unwavering support.

The first category includes M. J. Carlson, Darlene Gudea, Pete Blocksom, Brian and Jan Hieggelke, Carol Jackson, Jim and Peg Muntz, Gil Kaufman, Rob Feder, and Betsy Lancefield Lane. Historian Theodore H. White once said, "There are two kinds of editors: those who correct your copy and those who say it's wonderful." He obviously never met Betsy, who always manages to do both.

The second category is chock full of people, led by my wonderful family—especially fellow writers Emma, Frank Sr., Leslie, Michael, Pete, and Mary Lou, whom we will always miss.

Opposite Attractions

There are two kinds of people on this Earth: men and women. So when you get the perspective from both of them, it's just like a battle of the sexes.

—RAPPER LUDACRIS

There are only two kinds of people in the world: toxic and nourishing.

—INGRID CROCE, WIDOW OF SINGER JIM CROCE

There are two kinds of people in the world. One walks on the beach at twilight and looks out to sea, thinking profound thoughts. The other scans the windows of the beach houses, peering inside.

—AUTHOR CAROLYN SEE

There are two kinds of people that really know how to pray:

> those that have great faith and those that are truly desperate.
>
> —PARATROOPER AND CHAPLAIN MAJOR FRANK BRUNING

There are two kinds of people:

> those who stop at an accident and those who drive by.
>
> —MARLO THOMAS QUOTING HER FATHER, DANNY, IN THE BOOK *FATHERS*

There are two kinds of people:

> those who take things positively, and those who think pessimistically. Each group of people enjoy themselves in their own way.
>
> —NOBEL PRIZE–WINNING NOVELIST KENZABURO OE

There are two kinds of people:
> those who care and those who don't.
>
> —FOLKSINGER ARLO GUTHRIE

There are two kinds of people: givers and takers.
> The takers eat better, but the givers sleep better.
>
> —UNKNOWN

There are two kinds of people:
> those who laugh at their own jokes and those who don't.
>
> —THOMAS HURKA, WRITING IN THE *TORONTO GLOBE AND MAIL*

There are only two kinds of people in this world:
> those who pass on chain letters and those who think people who pass on

chain letters are the stupidest people
in the world.
—Syndicated columnist Roger Simon

There are two kinds of people:
there are people who are sure they're
going to win millions in the lottery
and there are people who are sure
nobody ever really does.
—Diane White, writing in the *Boston Globe*

There are two kinds of people:
the glommers and the people who
want their own space. Where you get
into trouble is a glommer married to
a non-glommer.
—Romance novelist Laurie Schnebly Campbell

There are two kinds of people in the world:
> those who, upon finding spiders,
> fearlessly give them their freedom,
> and those who annihilate them
> before they can attack.
>
> —VALERIE SCHOEN, WRITING IN THE *CHICAGO TRIBUNE*

There are two kinds of people in this world:
> those who count the days until
> December 25 and those who count
> the days until December 26.
>
> —LARENDA LYLES ROBERTS, WRITING IN THE *SAN FRANCISCO EXAMINER*

When it comes to Christmas, there are two kinds of people:
> those who live and plan for the
> holidays all year long (and have their
> house lights strung before the

Thanksgiving turkey is trimmed), and those who can never quite believe it's already that time of year again.

—KATHERINE SEIGENTHALER, WRITING IN THE *WASHINGTON POST*

When it comes to special occasions like Christmas, birthdays, and anniversaries, there are two kinds of people:

those who plan well in advance so there are no last-minute fiascos and those who consider long-term planning something done the night before an event, like me.

—CHRIS ZELKOVICH, WRITING IN THE *TORONTO STAR*

There are two kinds of people in this world: those who tear into their Christmas packages like wild hyenas and those who think it's better to give than to receive. The kids and I come down on the side of the hyenas. We tear into packages like they will disappear if we don't unwrap them fast enough. My wife, on the other hand, will be unwrapping presents until sometime in the new year. This has been a point of contention for us throughout our marriage.

—BILL NASH, WRITING IN THE *VENTURA COUNTY STAR*

There are two kinds of people in the world: those who want to know ahead of time what their Christmas present is and those who enjoy being surprised on Christmas morning. My wife and I are in the latter category. And if you are not, that's all right, too. It's a free country. If you are the kind of fool who wants to spoil Christmas for you and everyone else by behaving like a child and finding your present early, you will certainly hear no criticism from me.

—BILL HALL, WRITING IN THE LEWISTON, IDAHO, *MORNING TRIBUNE*

There are two kinds of people in the world: there are those who regard gloves as a way of keeping your hands warm, and those who see them as a fashion accessory.

—MILES KINGTON, WRITING IN THE *LONDON INDEPENDENT*

IT TAKES TWO

There are two kinds of people in the world: regular people, and people who plan out their next day's outfit before they go to sleep.

—JUDY MARKEY, WRITING IN THE *CHICAGO SUN-TIMES*

There are two kinds of people: those who keep their favorite T-shirts in heavy rotation and those who NEVER wear them.

—PAUL TURNER, WRITING IN THE *SPOKANE SPOKESMAN-REVIEW*

There are two kinds of people in the married world: those who leave their shoes in the middle of darkened hallways and those who trip over them headlong.

—CHRISTINE DRAKE, WRITING IN THE *ATLANTA JOURNAL-CONSTITUTION*

There are two kinds of people in this world: people who are compulsively on time and people who don't have the foggiest notion of what being on time means.

—MIMI STANG, WRITING IN THE *GREENSBORO NEWS & RECORD*

There are two kinds of people in the world: those who insist on lending books they like to their friends and promptly forget who has them, and those who borrow books and forget to return them.

—SID McKEEN, WRITING IN THE WORCESTER, MASSACHUSETTS, *SUNDAY TELEGRAM*

There are two kinds of writers: those that make you think, and those that make you wonder.

—NOVELIST BRIAN ALDISS

IT TAKES TWO

There are two kinds of people:
> those who read at the table and those who won't tolerate it. For it goes without saying that one doesn't merely abstain, oneself. That's not enough; one must keep everybody else from doing it.
>
> —MICHAEL KERNAN, WRITING IN THE *WASHINGTON POST*

There are two kinds of people in the world:
> those who read the funny papers and prize them with all their hearts and those who, tragically, do not.
>
> —JAY MAEDER, WRITING IN THE *CHICAGO TRIBUNE*

Why didn't anyone ever tell me that there are only two kinds of people in the world:
> newspaper savers and newspaper tossers? And why did they let me, a

sensible saver, plunge headlong into marriage with a fanatic tosser?

—NANCY C. HAUSWALD, WRITING IN THE *BALTIMORE SUN*

There are people who hope that Elvis is still alive
and there are people who are afraid he may be.

—DIANE WHITE, WRITING IN THE *BOSTON GLOBE*

There are two kinds of people in the world:
people who love Bon Jovi, and guys.

—DARRYL STERDAN, WRITING IN THE *WINNIPEG SUN*

I've only met two kinds of people:
those who whistle and those who try or have tried.

—OREGON'S WHISTLING MITCH HIDER, QUOTED BY UPI

There are two kinds of people:
> those who, when presented with the sheer inevitability of a chase scene, cringe, and those who sit up straighter in their seats as if bracing for impact.
> —KEVIN M. WILLIAMS, WRITING IN THE *CHICAGO SUN-TIMES*

There are two kinds of people in this world:
> those who forget the plot of this week's Cameron Diaz flick as soon as they leave the multiplex and those who can, with the least encouragement, recite at least half the dialogue of *Casablanca*.
> —CARLA LABUNSKI, WRITING IN THE *CHICAGO DAILY HERALD*

There are two kinds of people in the world:
> those who find *The Sound of Music* a lovable and inspiring show, and those

who think the musical is shallow, saccharine, and gaggingly cute.

—ROBERT FELDBERG, WRITING IN THE *BERGEN COUNTY RECORD*

I think there are two kinds of people in the world:

those who enjoy "Roadrunner" cartoons and those whose stomachs churn in frustration. The first kind laughs when the coyote plummets to the canyon floor; the second kind wants to scream, "Why does he keep buying those Acme products? Why can't he find some other animal to eat?" These two kinds of people are generally known, in the popular vernacular, as men and women.

—JOAN RYAN, WRITING IN THE *SAN FRANCISCO CHRONICLE*

IT TAKES TWO

Have you noticed that the human race is divided into two distinct, irreconcilable groups?

> Those who walk into rooms and automatically turn television sets on, and those who walk into rooms and automatically turn them off.
>
> —ACTOR LAURENCE HARVEY, IN THE 1962 FILM *THE MANCHURIAN CANDIDATE*

There are two kinds of people in this world:

> those who love public radio and those who don't even know it exists.
>
> —KITTY FELDE, WRITING IN THE *LOS ANGELES TIMES*

There are two kinds of people in the world:

> those who recognize "Monty Python's Flying Circus" as the most glorious, ingenious, wildly hilarious

creation in the history of television, and those who just don't get it.

—CLINT O'CONNOR, WRITING IN THE *CLEVELAND PLAIN DEALER*

There are two kinds of people in this world: Trekkies, and people with lives.

—FILM CRITIC M. FAUST, QUOTED IN THE *BUFFALO NEWS*

There are two kinds of people in the world: people who ought to be guests on "Springer" and people who belong in the audience.

—TELEVISION CRITIC TOM FERAN, WRITING IN THE *CLEVELAND PLAIN DEALER*

There are two kinds of people in the world: those who have already mentally worked out precisely what eight records they would take to a desert island but haven't even bothered to make a will, and those who have arranged things the other way round.

—MILES KINGTON, WRITING IN THE *LONDON INDEPENDENT*

There are two kinds of people on New Year's Eve:

those who smugly announce that they will do what they always do, which is have a simple dinner and watch a video, and the other kind, who go out every 31st of December just out of morbid curiosity to find out how awful it's going to be this time.

—ADAIR LARA, WRITING THE *SAN FRANCISCO CHRONICLE*

There are two kinds of people in this world:
> those who want to leave a party, and those who want to stay — and they always marry each other.
>
> —GENERAL MAURICE HIRSCH

New Year's Day is the ultimate morning after. On January 1 the world is divided into two kinds of people:
> those who celebrated injudiciously the night before and are paying for it, and those who did not and are pleased with their own temperance; that is, those who are facing a brand-new year with bright eyes and high hopes and those who are facing it with a growl of discomfort and a hangover.
>
> —ANNA QUINDLEN, WRITING IN THE *NEW YORK TIMES*

There are two kinds of people in this world: slobs and the people who clean up after them.

—Road-cleaning volunteer Jesus Pernas, quoted in *Florida Today*

There are two kinds of people in the world: those who wet their toothbrush before putting on the toothpaste and those who don't.

—Bill Flick, writing in the Bloomington, Illinois, *Pantagraph*

There are two kinds of people in this world: those who sit on the pot and those who get off it. In most cases, it's men who do the former, and women, the latter. . . . So, gents, what we women often wonder is not only why you love the loo, but also what it is you love to do on it. Maybe that's where you are now, whilst reading this.

—SANDY NAIMAN, WRITING IN THE *TORONTO SUN*

There are two kinds of people in the world:
there are those who cannot pass a mirror without stealing a look at themselves, and those who cannot pass a mirror without averting their eyes.

—MILES KINGTON, WRITING IN THE *LONDON INDEPENDENT*

There are two kinds of people who will spring big bucks for a makeup mirror that magnifies their faces.
The first are young models who need to cover every eyelash, shadow their cheekbones, define their lips, and sculpt their faces into visions of perfection for the camera. The

second group are women who, without their glasses, can't find their faces.

—SYNDICATED COLUMNIST ERMA BOMBECK

There are two kinds of people in the world: those who tolerate air-conditioning and those who worship it.

—ROB KASPER, WRITING IN THE *BALTIMORE SUN*

There are two kinds of people in the world, it sometimes seems: those that can't sleep unless the window shades are drawn tightly shut, and those that can't sleep unless they are open.

—TERRY MAROTTA, WRITING IN THE BANGOR, MAINE, *DAILY NEWS*

There are two kinds of people:

> the ones that like sleeping next to the wall, and the ones that like sleeping next to the people who push them off the bed.
>
> —SHORT-STORY WRITER ETGAR KERET

There are two kinds of people in the world:

> those who sleep *au naturel* and those who shiver at the thought. Whether you're a member of the buff brigade or pajama people may say something about how comfortable you are with your body and how intimate your relationship is with a partner.
>
> —NANCY J. WHITE, WRITING IN THE *TORONTO STAR*

There used to be two kinds of people in the world:

> naked people and people who covered themselves with fur or mud or maybe a few discreetly placed chickens. Today, there are hardly any chronically naked people left. That's because it was the people who covered their ugliness with clothing who found mates.
>
> —BILL HALL, WRITING IN THE LEWISTON, IDAHO, *MORNING TRIBUNE*

There are two kinds of people:

> those who like the bedclothes so tight that their feet can't move, and claustrophobic types who like to move around. The problem comes

when the two types end up under the same covers.

—BETH SCHWINN, WRITING IN THE *SAN FRANCISCO EXAMINER*

It turns out there are two kinds of people in this world:
> people who cringe at the thought of a foot massage and people who would run naked over hot coals to get one.
>
> —PAM THOMAS, WRITING IN THE *PROVIDENCE JOURNAL-BULLETIN*

There are two kinds of people in life.
> There are people who make great first impressions, and there are people who wear well.
>
> —U.S. SENATOR PHIL GRAMM

Love Connections

There are two kinds of relationships—
> those that fail, and those that are difficult.
>
> —Radio host Joe Frank

There are two kinds of people:
> those who love things and use people and those who love people and use things.
>
> —Psychiatrist Steve Warres, quoted in the *Baltimore Sun*

There are two kinds of people in the world:
> those who want someone else to rescue them from their demons and fill up the holes in their souls, and those who are committed to rescuing themselves and filling the holes in their own souls.
>
> —Syndicated astrologer Rob Brezsny

There really are two kinds of people: optimists and pessimists. There is something about being single, particularly when you reach a certain age, that turns naturally upbeat people into scrooges. You feel your life is not turning out the way it was supposed to and that sours your outlook. Also, single people develop an egocentric view of things. I suspect it comes from living alone and not having anyone around to validate your perceptions or tell you you're screwy.

—RUTHE STEIN, WRITING IN THE *SAN FRANCISCO EXAMINER*

At least once a week, I am rudely reminded that there are two kinds of people in the world:

> those who assume all single people are miserable, and those of us who are bewildered by the people who assume all singles are miserable.
>
> —SUSAN BARBIERI, WRITING IN THE *BERGEN COUNTY RECORD*

The world can be divided into two kinds of people:

> those who would take out a personal ad saying, "This is me, and I'd like to meet," and those who would rather stay at home alone—for an eternity—than do any such thing.
>
> —PAUL POVSE, WRITING IN THE SPRINGFIELD, ILLINOIS, *STATE JOURNAL-REGISTER*

A crowded world thinks aloneness is always loneliness and that to seek it is a perversion. It isn't. There are two kinds of people:

> those who prefer to be alone, at least occasionally, and those who can't stand being alone. The latter group also includes those who can't stand for other people to be alone and feel they must inflict their company on them.
>
> —UNIVERSITY OF CENTRAL ARKANSAS PROFESSOR W. C. JAMESON

When it comes to love, there are two kinds of people in this world:

> those who find it easily, and those who don't. For the first group, the course of true love is, indeed, very smooth.

They go to school, grow up, meet someone, fall in love, and are in turn desired by the beloved. Everything that follows fits like a glove. They marry, have children, and proceed to lead a generally angst-free existence. Theirs is a lucky, if uneventful, life.

For the other group, the path of love is full of twists and turns. These people have problems finding the right partner, yet they keep on searching, shifting between happiness and despair. . . . Looking for love might be a nerve-racking journey, but you will never find any of them complaining that their lives are dull.

—Sumiko Tan, writing in Singapore's *The Straits Times*

Two kinds of people attend high-school proms:

> preening popular types and geeks who lurk in the corners, wondering why their dates never returned from that "quick" trip to the rest room.
>
> —Syndicated columnist Tony Snow

For a seeker of true romance, there are two kinds of first dates:

> potentially life-changing or a waste of time.
>
> —Paul Turner, writing in the *Spokane Spokesman-Review*

Two kinds of people should be kept out of your dating Rolodex.

> The first is easy and obvious. Omit anyone who's married. But the second

is a bit more complicated, harder to recognize, and even more difficult to avoid. That's the person in between relationships, better known as the IBR. The IBR has recently severed a long-term or meaningful tie. Anyone dating an IBR automatically becomes a "TP"—Transitional Person.

When an IBR and a TP come together, they go straight to purgatory. That's where the IBR recovers and works out unresolved issues with the TP. The IBR emerges intact, after a few weeks or a few months, ready to pursue a heavenly relationship. Meanwhile, the TP is left behind, in an emotional heap. Some TPs then become IBRs. It's a vicious cycle.

—Laura Yee, writing in the *Cleveland Plain Dealer*

Those of you in your prime dating years may (falsely) believe that the world is filled with two kinds of people:

> couples, and single people who go out on dates in search of that special someone. In truth, the world is filled with three kinds of people: couples, single people who date, and single people who stay at home and eat microwave pizzas and watch "Eight Is Enough" reruns.
>
> —HUMORIST HEATHER HAVRILESKY, WRITING IN SUCK.COM

According to my mother, members of the opposite sex in her generation had two kinds of relationships:

> going steady or nothing at all. If she was friends with a boy, she was his

girlfriend. If she went out with a mixed group, every girl was coupled with a boy. Platonic friendships were reserved for people of the same sex.

The women's movement blurred those boundaries and opened the door for more diverse interactions between the sexes. I have guy friends I think of as brothers. I love talking with them, but I'd never want to be intimate with them. I also have had some guy friends, like the one I'm seeing now, turn into boyfriends.

—Elaine Williams, writing in the Lewiston, Idaho, *Morning Tribune*

There are two kinds of people on Valentine's Day.

> There are people in relationships, and people who hate people in relationships.
>
> —ROBERT MCNAMARA, WRITING IN THE SYRACUSE, NEW YORK, *POST-STANDARD*

There are two kinds of romance:

> obligatory romance and optional romance. Obligatory romance is celebrating birthdays, Christmas, and Valentine's Day. Optional is little surprises, such as champagne toasts, weekend getaways, and cards.
>
> —ARETHA FRISON, WRITING IN THE LAKELAND, FLORIDA, *LEDGER*

There are really only two kinds of people in the world:

> people with a flair for romance, and people who don't have a clue.
>
> —From "The L.A. Times Love Quiz," published in the *Los Angeles Times*

In the realm of Valentine's Day cards there are two types of people:

> those who buy short, pithy cards and those who go for the long and sappy ones. Spend enough time in the aisles of card shops, and you'll see it's mostly the men who pick out the syrupy ones. Given their one chance a year to lay bare their full emotions, men often go wild.
>
> —Abraham T. McLaughlin, writing in the *Christian Science Monitor*

There are two kinds of people in the world:
people who love doing things for the
first time and the rest of us — who
CANNOT WAIT FOR THE FIRST
TIME TO BE OVER, so we can be safe,
and familiar, and at the second time.
And I am not just talking about sex.
—JUDY MARKEY, WRITING IN THE *CHICAGO SUN-TIMES*

In our society, there's only two kinds of sex.
Either perfect sex or no sex at all.
—SEXOLOGIST JUDY SEIFER

Let's compare the two kinds of lovers.
The first type is a study in technique.
He views love as an act of sexuality; he
knows all the moves and has practiced
them from a mental place. But when the

physical act is over, both people are left feeling cold and empty. No connection has been made, because the main ingredient was left out: love. The second type of lover is all heart. He views love as a way of life. But this person has no idea how to touch his lover with enough sensitivity that she will be able to receive him. The concept is right, but once again, no connection is made. The true archetype of the lover merges technique with an open heart to connect with another human being.
—AUTHOR LYNN V. ANDREWS

There are two kinds of sex:
pornographic sex, and sex from the heart, the spirit.
—POET MICHAEL RYAN

There are two kinds of sex: classical and baroque. Classical sex is romantic, profound, serious, emotional, moral, mysterious, spontaneous, abandoned, focused on a particular person, and stereotypically feminine. Baroque sex is pop, playful, funny, experimental, conscious, deliberate, amoral, anonymous, focused on sensation for sensation's sake, and stereotypically masculine. The classical mentality taken to an extreme is sentimental and finally puritanical; the baroque mentality taken to an extreme is pornographic and finally obscene. Ideally, a sexual relation ought to create a satisfying tension between the two modes . . . or else blend them so well that the distinction disappears.

—AUTHOR ELLEN WILLIS

There are two kinds of people:
> those who think that sex is a gorgeous trick, and those who don't.
> —Heather Mallick, writing in the *Toronto Sun*

There are two kinds of love:
> sensual and sentimental. Sensual love has the present and little future only. The sentimental love has the present, past, and future, so it is more desirable. It will be slower but it will last longer.
> —Author Edward Leedskalnin

Could there be more than two kinds of love?
> How many are there? Well, that's sort of an unanswerable question.

One can evade these questions by giving smart answers, like as many kinds as there are different kinds of people, which may be the case.
—Playwright Tom Stoppard

There are two kinds of love.
Good and bad, or mature and immature. And you can't tell one from the other in the first few months.
—Author Sol Gordon

Only true love can lead to true happiness, but there are two kinds of love:
the love that cares for the other, like God's love for us; and the selfish love that cares more for oneself than the other, which is more appealing

but always ends in misery and disappointment.

—The Reverend Nicholas Maestrini

The Greeks recognized that there were two kinds of love,

> Common Love and Noble Love. The combination of these two loves will make for an everlasting love. It is the love of mind, body, and soul, not the foolish love of youth, or the love of intellect a person develops later in life.

—From PageWise.com

Most people will acknowledge that there are two kinds of love:

> one that is instantaneous, passionate, and undeniable, and one that is comfortable, controlled, and

companionable. Many of us search for the former but find the latter.

—Critic James Berardinelli

There are two kinds of love:
selfish and selfless love. Selfish love is conditional—you love on condition that your needs are met, and when your partner falls short of serving your needs, you may be tempted to reject them and search elsewhere. With conditional love, we see our partners as an extension of ourselves and feel that it is our responsibility to correct or change them. Although we constantly learn from each other, the role of a spouse is not that of an authority or a teacher, but that of an equal.

—Simon Jacobson, writing on MeaningfulLife.com

There are two kinds of love:
> the new or young love depicted in movies when one person asks, "Do you love me?" and the other answers, "I loooove you, I adore you, I love your hair, your eyes, your toenails. . . ." And there's the love depicted in *Fiddler on the Roof*, when Tevye asks his wife of twenty-five years, "Do you love me?" and she says, "Do I what?" (later adding reassuringly, "I suppose I do").
>
> —Barbara Klaus, writing in *Newsday*

There are two kinds of wedding dresses.
> The "Wow!" dress and the "Isn't-that-a-pretty-dress" dress.
>
> —Bridal consultant Dorothy Fey, quoted in the *St. Louis Post-Dispatch*

There are two kinds of marriages:
> where the husband quotes the wife and where the wife quotes the husband.
>
> —DRAMATIST CLIFFORD ODETS

Most of us were brought up to believe there was a single entity called a Good Husband. Yet there are actually two very different kinds of good husbands:
> the Boyfriend and the Husband. The former is everything you've wanted since you were fifteen: sexy, spontaneous, irresistible. He makes you laugh, makes you shiver, makes you mad as hell. The thing is, he never quite pictured himself as a husband and father, and deep down

he still doesn't. When you're trying to explain the concept of equal parenting or picking up his wet towels from the floor or refusing to sit through one more Jackie Chan video, you wonder: Did I make the biggest mistake of my life?

The Husband is your best buddy, a man you can count on to walk the baby at 3 A.M., research *Consumer Reports* for the safest car, hang up his shirts, and even buy you tampons on the way home. Yes, sex is more tender than thrilling, but isn't that to be expected with time? Still, sometimes you wonder if this cozy security is all it's cracked up to be. Shouldn't marriage have more pizzazz, electricity, mystery? Well, yes. And Boyfriend husbands should stay home more often, too. But just as there is no one good marriage, there is no one good husband.

—LESLEY DORMEN, WRITING IN *REDBOOK*

There are two kinds of husbands, the because ofs and the in spite ofs. The because ofs encourage their wives and help them meet their goals. The in spite ofs do not believe in their wives' abilities, forcing their spouses to show their husbands that they will, indeed, succeed.

—CLOTHING COMPANY FOUNDER LINDA HEIDENREICH, QUOTED IN THE *CHICAGO TRIBUNE*

Extensive research has proved conclusively that there are two kinds of husbands.

> One: the husband who takes absolutely no interest whatsoever in household affairs. And two: the husband whose wife wishes he'd mind his own business and leave things alone.
>
> —FROM A "FATHER KNOWS BEST" EPISODE FIRST BROADCAST JUNE 22, 1950

There are two kinds of marriage.

> It's high- or low-level marriage, and you're going to have to choose it. Low-level marriage means it's comfortable and convenient. High-level marriage means you come first. You don't go out without your spouse. The end.
>
> —AUTHOR DR. PAUL PEARSALL

There are two kinds of marriages:
bad marriages and hard marriages.

—EVANGELIST AND AUTHOR RICHARD EXLEY

There are people who think "Married… With Children" is a sitcom,
and there are people who know it's a documentary.

—DIANE WHITE, WRITING IN THE *BOSTON GLOBE*

There are two kinds of marriages:
selfish marriages and selfless marriages. In a selfish marriage, each party is constantly thinking, "What can I get out of it, what is he/she doing for me?" In a selfless marriage, the primary concern is pleasing the other partner, and in giving they receive so much.

—FROM *THE WEDDING COLLECTION* MAGAZINE

For both men and women, there are two kinds of affairs:

> the play-and-stay and the sex-that-wrecks. . . . The first kind of affair is intended to draw attention to problems in the existing relationship in the hope of addressing them. The second kind is intended to destroy the relationship.
>
> —KATHRYN HOLMQUIST, WRITING IN THE *IRISH TIMES*

To cheat on your spouse at this moment in history is to run the risk of killing your family. . . . There's no such thing as safe sex. There are only two kinds of people:

> the healthy and the sick. The healthy have to stay that way, and the sick should be treated with compassion.
>
> —PSYCHIATRIST AND TALK-SHOW HOST DR. DAVID VISCOTT

You need two kinds of people to create a battering relationship—

a male for whom domination and control are a personality pattern, usually as a response of his own sense of inadequacy and his own passivity. And by luck or design—usually by luck—this male meets his female counterpart, a person who feels inadequate, who invites control and is willing to lose control over her life for the security and comfort of having someone show her the right way to live. Now, there's nothing wrong with trade-offs in long-term relationships, but trading off pain or lack of selfhood for the sake of security is pathological.

—Psychiatrist Samuel C. Klagsbrun, quoted in *Mirabella*

There are two kinds of divorce.

One is the child-free divorce, a relatively simple affair involving two consenting adults hurting each other, or maybe one consenting adult hurting the other. A contract is dissolved, a vow is broken, and the promised future splinters. There is usually much rage and anguish, but only two people are directly involved (even the common third person in the divorce hovers on the margins of the severed marriage), and in this sense it is like the end of any kind of important affair, but with strings attached.

And then there is the divorce where a child or children are involved. Here are problems squared and pain to the power of ten. If child-free divorce unties the knot, family divorce tears at a whole tapestry of relationships.

—NICCI GERRARD, WRITING IN THE *LONDON OBSERVER*

There are only two kinds of love stories in the world:

boy loses girl; girl loses boy. You're gonna die in your own arms.

—ACTOR ANTHONY LAPAGLIA IN THE 2000 FILM *AUTUMN IN NEW YORK*

There are two kinds of love:

our love and God's love. But God makes both kinds.

—ANONYMOUS

There are two kinds of people in the world:

> the givers and the takers. A marriage between two givers can be a beautiful thing. Friction is inevitable for a giver and a taker. Two takers can claw each other to pieces within a period of weeks.
>
> —Syndicated columnist Dr. James Dobson

There are two kinds of couples who go the distance:

> those who grow together, at a similar rate and in a similar direction, and those who are too stunted to walk out the door.
>
> —Carolyn Hax, writing in the *Toronto Star*

In this world, there are two kinds of people:

> the dumpers and the dumped.
>
> —CRITIC JOHN GREEN, WRITING IN *BOOKLIST*

There are two kinds of people in this world,

> and you ain't one of them!
>
> —DOLLY PARTON TO HER ON-SCREEN MANAGER IN THE 1984 FILM *RHINESTONE*

There are two kinds of lovers in this world:

> those who like diamonds and those who like dirt.
>
> —SONGWRITERS GRANT MCLENNAN AND ROBERT FORSTER

There are two kinds of people in the world:

> people who wish they were married, and people who wish they were single.
>
> —*WASHINGTON POST* READER TOM WITTE

There are two kinds of relationships in life. There are those bound by contract of some sort; be it blood ties, marriage vows, parental responsibilities, legal contracts, terms of employment, and so on. Friendship, on the other hand, is voluntary and mutual. Friendship has the potential for rising above the trials of life whereas, as painful experience often proves, relationships of the other kind may only be glued together by the blood tie, the agreement and the covenant—the love which might have provided a more enduring cement is lacking.

—Chaplain Robin Giles, writing in e-Milestones

There are two kinds of love.

> There's the kind where you're so happy together, you can't be apart. And then, there's the other kind that is more painful; it's not that you're truly happy together, it's just that you're more miserable apart.
>
> —MIKE KURTIS, WRITING ON MR.CRANKY.COM

There are two kinds of love.

> One says plainly, "I love you. I give myself to you." The other says, "I love myself and I want you; I need you; you please me. I like what you can do for me." This second kind is always temporary. There will come a time when you displease me and I won't want you.
>
> —D. L. DYKES JR., IN *THE POWER OF LOVE*

There are two kinds of love:
> one that follows the mechanisms of jealousy, and one that follows the mechanisms of best friendship.
>
> —GERMAN WRITER SERGE KREUTZ

It seems to me that there are two kinds of love.
> One is generous in its impulse; the lovers reach out and embrace the world, too. The other kind turns in jealously on itself, almost as if love were an anti-social act, a seceding from the environment. The second kind is more common.
>
> —NOVELIST AND CRITIC ANATOLE BROYARD

There are two kinds of love, I believe.
There is first love, and that comes to you only through the emotions. It is a dream, a song heard far away. There is no thought to it, thinking doesn't enter into it at all. There is no conscious planning about it. Marriage doesn't seem to be the natural culmination of it because marriage is planning and thinking ahead. And then it leaves you, eventually, because it has never been quite real. You never really touch it with your hands. And it leaves you without bitterness until you grow old enough to realize that first things never come again.

There is second love, or I hope there is. There are probably several kinds of love, really. I am not one of those who believe that there is only one love in a lifetime. We all have many different friends, for instance, and we give them different things of ourselves. Each friend evokes a different reaction. Loves are like that, too—we may love one man one way and another man quite another way—but second love is apt to last longer, I believe. It is more apt to be based on sound, substantial things. Common tastes and interests, common friends and plans and ambitions. It is durable. It is not a dream.

—Silent-film star Janet Gaynor

There are two kinds of love:

> love for its own pleasure, or love for the sake of another; the first is carnal love, the second is spiritual. Carnal love knows the other person only in a biological moment. Spiritual love knows the other person at all moments. In erotic love, the burdens of the other are regarded as impairing one's own happiness; in spiritual love, the burdens of others are opportunities for service.

—CATHOLIC BISHOP FULTON J. SHEEN

There are two kinds of love:

> physical and spiritual. One cannot live or survive without the other, as

two lovers cannot survive without each other.

—From Lovingyou.com

There are two kinds of love.
There is benign love and there is malignant love.

—Playwright Tennessee Williams

There are two kinds of love:
the intrinsic, calm love that we feel for people to whom we're related by birth; and the more intimate, fiery love that exists in marriage. . . . The love within a family, between relatives who are born of the same flesh, is innate. . . . The love between a husband and wife isn't like that. Their love wasn't always

there; they didn't always know each other; they weren't always related. No matter how well they get to know one another, they aren't alike. They are different from each other physically, emotionally, and mentally. They love each other in spite of the differences and because of them, but there isn't enough of a commonality between them to create a casual, calm love. The differences remain even after they are married, and the love between them will have to overcome these differences.

—AUTHOR AND RABBI MANIS FRIEDMAN

There are two kinds of love in this world. There is the love associated with peace, respect, and goodwill, which

IT TAKES TWO

is like brotherly love, something the world is really in need of. Then there's the other kind of love, romantic love that can go on breaking hearts.

—Chan Wai Kong, writing in the *London Sunday Mail*

Due to the fact there are two kinds of love, you will always have two kinds of lovers.
The person you can talk with, care about, and who gives you a good time. And the person who makes you laugh and cry, makes you feel you're the greatest person on earth. Just make sure you pick out the right one to share your life with.

—Author Sandra Bleijerveld

There are two kinds of love.

One is where your heart beats fast and you're addicted to the other person. Then there's the other kind, when you cherish someone, and they move you by their courage and their personality and things like that. There is still an attraction, a motive of the heart, but it doesn't have the same kind of urgency. There's another part of your brain at work. This is a long-distance kind of love that has to take over in a marriage, or there is no marriage. It involves sticking with the other person and loving them through the bumps.

—ACTOR ALAN ALDA

If one wished to be perfectly sincere, one would have to admit there are two kinds of love:

> well-fed and ill-fed. The rest is pure fiction.
>
> —FRENCH NOVELIST COLETTE

Friendships and Family Affairs

It has been said that there are two kinds of friends:

> friends of time and friends of the mind. The first—pals from the old neighborhood, summer camp, our first job—give our lives continuity; the second—soul mates who share our interests, values, goals—give our lives possibility. Both stir our capacity to care and connect.
>
> —Oprah Winfrey

There are two kinds of people in this world:

> elevator people and basement people. Elevator people bring you up, basement people bring you down. Surround yourself with the former.
>
> —Real estate consultant Blake Hutcheson, quoted in the *Toronto Globe and Mail*

In the end, there are only two kinds of friends:

> the true and the false.
>
> —MANUEL LAZARO, WRITING IN THE *MANILA BULLETIN*

There are two kinds of people in the world:

> people who remember their friends' birthdays, and the rest of us.
>
> —JUDY MARKEY, WRITING IN THE *CHICAGO SUN-TIMES*

There are two kinds of friends:

> friends of the road and friends of the heart. Friends of the road are people who pass through your life. You don't know them forever. If you lose contact, you lose the friendship because contact is what keeps it alive. Friends of the heart are

different. It's like family — long-lived and continuous. There is absolute trust and the friendship is fully reciprocal. You don't have to be there all the time to maintain the friendship. Friends of the road may be shallower, but they are valuable because they provide us with a kaleidoscope of changing patterns in our lives.

—AUTHOR LILLIAN RUBIN

There are two kinds of people in the world: those who come into a room and say, "Here I am!" and those who come in and say, "Ah, there you are!"

—UNKNOWN

There are two kinds of people in the world: people who have secrets and people who have "boundary problems"— they share everything.

—BARBARA BROWN, WRITING IN THE *ANCHORAGE DAILY NEWS*

There are two kinds of people who blow through life like a breeze. And one kind is gossipers, and the other kind is gossipees.

—HUMORIST OGDEN NASH

My mother once said to me that there are two kinds of people, ulcer-givers and ulcer-getters. And my grandmother used to say to me, "It's better to give than to receive."

—JUDGE JUDY SHEINDLIN

There are two kinds of people in this world.

> First, touchy-feelies, the ones who ask you how you feel, and when you say fine, they grab you by the forearm, look at you with concern and say, "How do you really feel?" Then there are the people who can't even say the L-word to their own mothers, as in "I l--- you." I'm in that category.
>
> —MARK PATINKIN, WRITING IN THE *PROVIDENCE JOURNAL-BULLETIN*

There are two kinds of people that I can recognize now.

> There are the ones who had a male and a female who were in charge of their lives and attended to them, and validated them and nurtured them

and became like a microcosm of the world for that person before the age of nine. If you don't have those people, you end up with a hole that you're trying to fill for the rest of your life.

—Music legend Quincy Jones

There are two kinds of families.
One where a child is reading and the father says, "Have you nothing else to do?" The other kind where the child is not reading and they say, "Have you nothing to read?" I was clearly in the second.

—European Bank President Jacques Attali

In family photos, I like the ones where everyone's normal except for the one person who's got a Mohawk or two thousand piercings—the freak. I love that. It makes you go, "Well yeah, OK, that's Carol." In high school I noticed that there were two kinds of families:

> the ones where all the kids looked the same, and the ones where the kids looked different. It actually seemed like the families who all looked different were smarter.
>
> —NOVELIST DOUGLAS COUPLAND

There are two kinds of people in the world:

> parents and their former friends who don't have—and may not want—kids.
>
> —HELAINE R. FREEMAN, WRITING IN THE *ARKANSAS DEMOCRAT-GAZETTE*

In the end there are only two kinds of people:

> those who have children and those who do not. Being a parent is another dimension of joy and pain, not always in that order.
>
> —SYNDICATED COLUMNIST RICHARD REEVES

There are two kinds of parents in this world.

> There are those who sit on the edge of the pool during swimming lessons, cheering their kid's progress and generally interfering with the instructor's plan. Then there are those who sit in chairs against the wall, reading, doing paperwork, and generally ignoring what's happening right in front of them.
>
> —LINDA BAKER, WRITING IN THE *PORTLAND OREGONIAN*

IT TAKES TWO

There are two kinds of parents.
There are parents who swear that every moment they spend with their kids is a priceless gem to be stored forever in their bank vault of memories. And then there are honest parents. Honest parents are the ones who admit that they could survive an hour or two without phones ringing, TVs blasting, and refrigerator doors hanging open. They're the ones for whom the patter of little feet is starting to sound like an endless stampede. Honest parents love their children, too. But they're not trying to kid anybody. There are times when they would trade an internal organ for twenty minutes of peace and quiet.

—SYNDICATED COLUMNIST D. L. STEWART

The world is full of two kinds of people:

> those who are perennially prompt
> and those who are congenitally late.
> The latter are called parents.
> —SYNDICATED COLUMNIST MARY MCCARTY

At the end of ten straight days of Christmas vacation, there are two kinds of parents:

> the quick, and the ones pouring
> apple juice all day long.
> —SYNDICATED COLUMNIST TONY KORNHEISER

I read in a Reader's Digest article that there are two kinds of mothers:

> those who put their child's flowers
> in a milk bottle on top of the fridge,
> and those who put them in a vase on
> a piano. I'm a third kind:

IT TAKES TWO

I absentmindedly toss them in the trash, where the kids find them, and squawk.

—Adair Lara, writing in the *San Francisco Chronicle*

There are two kinds of moms in this world: those who are slingers and those who are sentimentalists. You've got your moms who, every couple of years, go into their kids' rooms and callously toss out mounds of toys and dreck in order to clear some space for all the new toys and new dreck. And you've got your moms who, unable to separate themselves from even the smallest bit of kid-related property, manage over the years to create a virtual memorabilia-crammed shrine to that self same kid.

—Judy Markey, writing in the *Chicago Sun-Times*

Everyone knows that there are two kinds of mothers in life:

wonderful and fabulous.

—Jay Stone, writing in the *Calgary Herald*

There are two kinds of mothers in this world.

The first kind can tell you the day before what she's serving for dinner tomorrow. The rest of us aren't sure exactly what will be on the table until we've checked what's inside that container at the back of the refrigerator shelf.

—Teryl Zarnow, writing in the *Orange County Register*

Did you ever witness pure devotion? That goo-goo, ga-ga kind of goofy devotion? Grown-ups let that sap spill out for just two kinds of people:

> babies and teen idols.
>
> —SYNDICATED COLUMNIST JAN TUCKWOOD

There are two kinds of kids:

> the ones that walk through the mud,
> and the ones that walk around it.
>
> —COLLEGE STUDENT JEFF SCHOETTLIN, QUOTED IN THE *CHRISTIAN SCIENCE MONITOR*

There are two kinds of kids:

> the ones who will tell you more than you want to know about everything,
> and the ones who tell you nothing.
>
> —SUSAN REIMER, WRITING IN THE *BALTIMORE SUN*

There are two kinds of grandparents:
grandpas and grandmas. Grandpa is the one with bald hair. Grandma is the one who brings us cookies.

—LORI, AGE FIVE, QUOTED IN THE *CHICAGO DAILY HERALD*

There are two kinds of people in the world:
those who thought their loved ones would never die, and those who no longer had any doubt.

—NOVELIST JON KATZ

There are two kinds of people in this world:
those who are generous of spirit and those who aren't. You can't tell which is which by the money they have, or their education or good

manners. You'll never recognize them by the kind of car they drive, the grammar they use, or the clothes they wear. You can spot a generous spirit by the amount of bread they throw on the water without expecting any of it to float back. Generous spirits don't keep score. They don't just remember you on your birthday. Generous spirits are never afraid that, by giving, they'll lose what they have.

—Syndicated columnist Tad Bartimus

Married to the Job

IT TAKES TWO

There are two kinds of people: workhorses and show horses.

—FORMER PRESIDENT HARRY S TRUMAN

My grandfather once told me that there are two kinds of people: those who do the work and those who take the credit. He told me to try to be in the first group; there was less competition there.

—INDIRA GANDHI

There are two kinds of people: those who sound the fire gong and those who climb up and down the ladder rescuing people from burning buildings.

—FORMER NEW YORK GOVERNOR HUGH L. CAREY

There are two kinds of people.

> There are the kinds of leaders who get a job done, and there are the kind that want to be seen doing it.
>
> —SPOKANE CITY COUNCILWOMAN PHYLLIS HOLMES, QUOTED IN THE *SPOKANE SPOKESMAN-REVIEW*

There are only two kinds of people on earth today . . .

> the people who lift and the people who lean.
>
> —POET ELLA WHEELER WILCOX

There are two kinds of people.

> Some like to run things. Some like to build things.
>
> —ADVERTISING EXECUTIVE JERRY I. REITMAN, QUOTED IN THE *NEW YORK TIMES*

IT TAKES TWO

There are two kinds of people:
the kind who sign the front of the paycheck and the kind who sign the back.

—ROY JAY, PRESIDENT OF THE AFRICAN AMERICAN CHAMBER OF COMMERCE OF OREGON, QUOTED IN THE *PORTLAND OREGONIAN*

There are two kinds of people in one's life:
people whom one keeps waiting, and the people for whom one waits.

—AUTHOR AND DRAMATIST SAMUEL NATHANIEL BEHRMAN

There are only two kinds of managers.
There are the highly effective ones, who the employees hate. And there are the ineffective ones who the employees might like. You only have a choice of

being a failure that people like or a success that people hate.

—DILBERT CREATOR SCOTT ADAMS

There are two kinds of people in this world.
There are the ones that say, "Pay me, and I'll do it." And there are the ones that say, "Let me do it, and I'll get paid eventually."

—FINANCIAL CONSULTANT DIANE WINN, QUOTED IN THE SOUTH BEND, INDIANA, *TRIBUNE*

There are two kinds of people in all companies:
those who can contribute to income and those who cost the company money. Hiring officials want to know which one you are.

—CAREER CONSULTANT THOMAS W. MORRIS III, QUOTED IN THE *WASHINGTON TIMES*

IT TAKES TWO

There are only two kinds of people who do not commit mistakes:
> those who have not yet been born
> and those who are already dead.
>
> —LATE MOZAMBIQUE PRESIDENT SAMORA MACHEL

There are two kinds of people:
> those who need security and a
> predictable situation; and those who
> demand challenge and a chance at
> the top job.
>
> —AUTHOR ROBERT TOWNSEND, IN *FURTHER UP THE ORGANIZATION*

There are two kinds of people:
> the ones who say they love their jobs
> and the ones who tell the truth.
>
> —RON GIVENS, WRITING IN THE *NEW YORK DAILY NEWS*

There are two kinds of people in business: one who works from home and the other who wants to.

—BUSINESSMAN STEVE LANG, QUOTED IN *DENVER BUSINESS JOURNAL*

There are two kinds of people: those who consider a rubber band an office supply and those who consider it a weapon.

—JON W. SPARKS, WRITING IN THE *MEMPHIS COMMERCIAL APPEAL*

There are two kinds of people in the world: those who keep their desks neat and those who keep them messy, and the first group is forever making the second feel guilty.

—CHERYL LAVIN, WRITING IN THE *CHICAGO TRIBUNE*

IT TAKES TWO

There are two kinds of people in this world: healthy ones with messy desks and neurotic ones with neat desks.

—MARK PATINKIN, WRITING IN THE *HOUSTON CHRONICLE*

There are two kinds of people: there are people who know whether they're left-brained or right-brained and there are people who feel lucky to have any brain at all.

—DIANE WHITE, WRITING IN THE *BOSTON GLOBE*

In the twenty-first century our society is going to belong to people who can work with information and manage it and think well. We are going to have two kinds of people, I suspect:

> those who manage information and those who are unemployed.
>
> —SCHOOL REFORM LEADER PHILLIP SCHLECHTY, QUOTED IN THE *ST. PETERSBURG TIMES*

There are two kinds of people in this world.

> Phone slaves, and phone masters.
>
> —TERRY BIBO, WRITING IN THE PEORIA, ILLINOIS, *JOURNAL STAR*

There are two kinds of people:

> those who cannot resist answering a ringing phone, and those who will wriggle all over with happiness to ignore it.
>
> —JOAN FRANK, WRITING IN THE *CHICAGO TRIBUNE*

IT TAKES TWO

There are two kinds of people in this world: those who use Macs, and those who are forced to use PCs.

—TOM REGAN, WRITING IN THE *CHRISTIAN SCIENCE MONITOR*

There are two kinds of people: Mac users and those waiting on hold for the help desk.

—S. B. CRAWFORD, WRITING IN THE AUGUSTA, GEORGIA, *CHRONICLE*

When it comes to computers and access to the Internet, there are two kinds of people: those who babble, and those who don't listen.

—C. W. NEVIUS, WRITING IN THE *SAN FRANCISCO CHRONICLE*

The world is divided into two kinds of people:

> techies who embrace computer technology and want more of it, and technophobes who loathe the idea of computers running their lives.
>
> —LORNA WILLIAMS, WRITING IN *FORBES*

There are two kinds of people:

> human beings and women—and when women ask that they be treated as human beings, they are accused of wanting to be men.
>
> —WRITER SIMONE DE BEAUVOIR

I'm only interested in two kinds of people:

> those who can entertain me, and those who can advance my career.
>
> —ACTRESS INGRID BERGMAN

The feminine revolution took two kinds of people.

> Some pointed out the problem to the Establishment, and then others were ready to step into the jobs that were created. I was one of those.
>
> —U.S. Astronaut Shannon Lucid

There are two kinds of people who ride the subway:

> those who push and those who get pushed. People who push get to live a lot longer than those who get pushed.
>
> —Syndicated columnist Art Buchwald

There are two kinds of people:

> those who walk into waiting elevators without breaking stride and

those of us who have summoned those very elevators by impatiently and repeatedly pressing the buttons.

—John Anders, writing in the *Dallas Morning News*

There are two kinds of people in the world: cannibals and lunch.

—Playwright Eric Overmyer

There are two kinds of people. There are those who look through a full appointment book and think of themselves as successful. And there are the really successful who see an empty page and say "Whoopee!"

—Photographer and children's book author Jill Krementz

There are two kinds of people in this world:
> those who work until they retire, and those who retire and go back to work until they're put in a box.
>
> —GOLF SHOP PROPRIETOR HENRY THOMAS, QUOTED IN THE *NEW ORLEANS TIMES-PICAYUNE*

There are two kinds of people in our world today:
> the happy and the informed.
>
> —DALE TURNER, WRITING IN THE *SEATTLE TIMES*

There are two kinds of people:
> those who speculate, and those who know. The latter group is much less likely to volunteer information. But they will sometimes tell you what you need to know, if you have established yourself as someone who is discreet.
>
> —LONA O'CONNOR, WRITING IN THE *CINCINNATI ENQUIRER*

There are two kinds of people in a crisis.
> There are those who know, but can't talk. And those who talk, but don't know.
>
> —FORMER IRANIAN HOSTAGE COLONEL CHARLES SCOTT, QUOTED IN THE *INDIANAPOLIS NEWS*

There are two kinds of people who don't say much:
> those who are quiet and those who talk a lot.
>
> —SMILEY ANDERS, WRITING IN THE BATON ROUGE, LOUISIANA, *MORNING ADVOCATE*

There are only two kinds of people in the stock market—
> those who have been terribly wrong in their short-term predictions and the liars.
>
> —FINANCIAL GURU LOUIS RUKEYSER

In my business, there are two kinds of people:

> those who make money and those who critique those who make money. I am proud to be in the former, and I will not let the latter stop me.
>
> —THESTREET.COM COFOUNDER JAMES CRAMER

There are two kinds of people in the world:

> those who, when taking money from a bank [ATM], carefully count it before putting it away, and those who put it away immediately, as if they can't quite believe they've actually been given it and there is a risk of their being asked for it back if they leave it in their hands for a moment longer.
>
> —MILES KINGTON, WRITING IN THE *LONDON INDEPENDENT*

Two kinds of people are most likely to try to cheat the IRS:

> those who don't make very much money and those who make a lot.
>
> —DOUGLAS B. FEAVER, WRITING IN THE *WASHINGTON POST*

There are two kinds of people:

> those who fill out their own tax forms and those who hand them over to someone who actually knows math.
>
> —SHAWN HUBLER, WRITING IN THE *LOS ANGELES TIMES*

There are two kinds of people I deplore in the teaching profession.

> One is the misfit who sneaks in to escape his inadequacy elsewhere and

IT TAKES TWO

who ought to be booted out — and isn't very often; and the other is the aggressive pest whose one purpose is to upset other people's applecarts, and the more apples the better.

—NOVELIST BERNARD MALAMUD

There are two kinds of people that come to trade shows.

There are what we call "tire kickers," who come for entertainment and to kick a few tires. Then there are "power buyers"—the ones with the influence to buy something.

—THOMAS LEMERY, CO-OWNER OF CREATACOR INC., QUOTED IN *CAPITAL DISTRICT BUSINESS REVIEW*

There are two kinds of lawyers:
> those who know the law and those who know the judge.
>
> —UNKNOWN

There are two kinds of people you never argue with:
> a cop on the street and a judge in a courtroom.
>
> —TOM MORAN, WRITING IN THE *HOUSTON CHRONICLE*

There are two kinds of people in prison:
> those who should never have been sent there, and those who should never be let out.
>
> —PLAYWRIGHT GEORGE BERNARD SHAW

Embracing Opportunity

IT TAKES TWO

There are two kinds of people in this world:
those who talk about it and those who do it.

—MANAGEMENT GURU TOM PETERS

There are only two kinds of people:
eagles and mosquitoes. You can either fly with the eagles or swarm with the mosquitoes.

—CAREER AND IMAGE CONSULTANT CAMILLE LAVINGTON, QUOTED IN THE *Chicago Tribune*

There are two kinds of people in this world:
those who are going to do something and those who actually do it.

—SYNDICATED COLUMNIST THOMAS SOWELL

There are two kinds of people in the world:
the Doers and the Viewers. The Doers thrust themselves into life

with enthusiasm. The Viewers have reduced life to a spectator sport. They don't even know what they're missing, and I'm sorry for them.

—SHIRLEY REDMOND, WRITING IN THE *CHRISTIAN SCIENCE MONITOR*

There are two kinds of people:
participants and observers. If you're a participant, you are going to fail, and I guarantee you're going to have a life of experience and joys and highs, and you'll be able to measure them. If you are an observer, you've got no business opening your mouth about anything. And if you do, your obligation is to be more gentle because you do not have a full grasp of what it takes.

—ACTOR KEVIN COSTNER

IT TAKES TWO

It is my experience from high school days in the not-so-distant past that there are two kinds of people that sit in the back row of a classroom:

> those who sleep and those who like to blow things up.
>
> —JAVIER SALONO, WRITING IN THE *ORLANDO SENTINEL*

There are two kinds of people:

> the ones who went to Woodstock, and the ones who wish they did. I definitely want to be one of the people who was there.
>
> —COMPUTER EXECUTIVE C. RUDY PURYEAR, QUOTED IN *FORBES*

There are two kinds of people in this world: those who are brilliant and shine immediately and then the rest of us who have to work for it.

—British TV talk-show host Lowri Turner

Perhaps there are two kinds of people: first are those whose lives unfold before them in an ascending line, moving from strength to strength, according to plan. I think very few are in this category. Or maybe they are a mirage. And then there are the rest of us who feel our way in the dark.

—Eleanor Mallett, writing in the *Cleveland Plain Dealer*

There are two kinds of people in life: those who spring from the womb knowing what they are going to do, and the rest of us who flounder.

—Humorist Margo Kaufman, quoted in the *Portland Oregonian*

There are two kinds of people in life: those who get stomped on and those who do the stomping.

—Comedian Norm Macdonald, in the 1998 film *Dirty Work*

There are two kinds of people in the world. Some people have guns. Other people dig.

—Actor Clint Eastwood, in the 1966 film *The Good, The Bad, and The Ugly*

There are two kinds of people:

> there are people who consult mental health professionals and there are people who don't, but probably ought to.
>
> —DIANE WHITE, WRITING IN THE *BOSTON GLOBE*

There are two kinds of people:

> those who have ideas, and those who can recognize them.
>
> —MATHWORKS, INC. CEO JACK LITTLE, QUOTED IN THE *BOSTON GLOBE*

There are two kinds of people:

> those who shine in the spotlight and those who shrink from it.
>
> —KENT YOUNGBLOOD, WRITING IN THE *WISCONSIN STATE JOURNAL*

There are two kinds of people in this world. Those who blow out everybody else's candle to make theirs shine brighter, and those who light everybody else's candle to make the world shine brighter. Which person do you want to be?

—TACOMA, WASHINGTON, RESIDENT JOE ESTEY, QUOTED IN THE *TACOMA NEWS TRIBUNE*

There are two kinds of people: ones that are bought . . . and the buyers.

—PLAYWRIGHT TENNESSEE WILLIAMS IN *ORPHEUS DESCENDING*

There are two kinds of people in the world. There are those who dream and follow their dreams, and those who dream and follow other people's dreams.

—Graphic designer Robin Axtell, quoted in the *Hartford Business Ledger*

There are two kinds of failures: the man who will do nothing he is told, and the man who will do nothing else.

—Author Perle Thomson

There are two kinds of failures: those who thought and never did, and those who did and never thought.

—*Peter Principle* author Laurence J. Peter

There are two kinds of people: those who blame the world for denying them, and those who find a way.

—Mark Patinkin, writing in the *Providence Journal-Bulletin*

IT TAKES TWO

Sometimes it seems that there are two kinds of people in this world:
> "can dos" and "yes, buts."
>
> —RICHARD LOUV, WRITING IN THE *SAN DIEGO UNION-TRIBUNE*

There are two kinds of people in the world:
> those that want things to go on exactly as they always have, and those who, when things aren't working, grab on to opportunities.
>
> —ADVERTISING EXECUTIVE GENE PETRUS, QUOTED IN *BUSINESS CLEVELAND*

I'm a member of that half of the human race which is inclined to divide the human race into two kinds of people.
> My dividing line runs between the people who crave certainty and the people who trust chance.
>
> —TECHNOLOGY GURU JOHN PERRY BARLOW, WRITING IN *WHOLE EARTH REVIEW*

There are those who want to be somebody, and those who want to do something.
> I am one of those who want to do something.
>
> —JEAN MONNET, FATHER OF THE EUROPEAN COMMON MARKET

There are two kinds of people in this world:
> the movers and shakers and those who get moved and shaken.
>
> —CLARENCE PAGE, WRITING IN THE *CHICAGO TRIBUNE*

There are two kinds of people:
> those who think they can, and those who think they can't, and they're both right.
>
> —HENRY FORD

Whine and Dine

There are two kinds of people in the world: those who understand that the only pizza worth eating comes on a thin, crisp crust — and those who have no taste at all.

—FOOD CRITIC RUTH REICHL, WRITING IN THE *LOS ANGELES TIMES*

There are two kinds of people in the world: those who always keep a bottle of champagne in the fridge, and those who don't. The former delight in life's possibilities, knowing an event that calls for the celebratory sparkle of champagne may be right around the corner. They are people worth cultivating. As for the others, they're a more deprived lot, not least because they end up drinking a lot less champagne.

—BEPPI CROSARIOL, WRITING IN THE *TORONTO GLOBE AND MAIL*

There are two kinds of drinkers.
One holes in some place and stays put to do his drinking. The other kind ambles.

—NOVELIST FREDRIC BROWN, WRITING IN *THE FABULOUS CLIPJOINT*

There are two kinds of people:
those who like food to melt in the mouth and those who like food to fight back.

—IRENE SAX, WRITING IN *NEWSDAY*

The world is divided into two kinds of people—

> those who don't grow basil and those who make pesto.
>
> —ADRIENNE COOK, WRITING IN THE *WASHINGTON POST*

There are two kinds of people:

> those who love garlic and those who loathe it. There's no middle of the road.
>
> —GARLIC GROWER WENDY DOUGLAS, QUOTED IN THE *CLEVELAND PLAIN DEALER*

There are two kinds of people in the world:

> chocoholics and aliens.
>
> —CAROL HORTON, WRITING IN THE *VIRGINIAN-PILOT AND LEDGER-STAR*

There are two kinds of [women] in the world:

> those who love chocolate . . . and bitches.
>
> —GREETING-CARD WRITER LESLIE MOAK MURRAY

There are two kinds of people in this world:

> those who share food and those who don't. Unlike oil and vinegar, the two often don't mix. Especially at restaurants.
>
> —NELSON PRICE, WRITING IN THE *INDIANAPOLIS NEWS*

If you've ever taken a long road trip, you know there are two kinds of people.

> There are the ones who will pull off the highway only when they see an exit

IT TAKES TWO

sign promising a nationally advertised fast-food chain, and then there are the ones willing to drive thirty miles out of their way to find a restaurant reputed to have the best clam chowder (or ribs or Key lime pie) in the state.

—PARRY GETTELMAN, WRITING IN THE *ORLANDO SENTINEL*

There are two kinds of people in the world:

those who decide at six that they want to go to dinner at seven, and those who reserved tonight's table sometime last month.

—FOOD CRITIC RUTH REICHL, WRITING IN THE *LOS ANGELES TIMES*

There are two kinds of people in this world:
> those who like to entertain in the kitchen and those who would just die if guests walked into that room.
>
> —JILL SELL, WRITING IN THE *CLEVELAND PLAIN DEALER*

There are two kinds of people,
> the ones who like to cook and the ones who like to clean.
>
> —MICHAEL KERNAN, WRITING IN THE *WASHINGTON POST*

The world is divided into two kinds of people:
> those who use coasters and those who don't.
>
> —JURA KONCIUS, WRITING IN THE *WASHINGTON POST*

There are two kinds of people in this world: those who carefully arrange plates, cups, and utensils in the dishwasher and those who load dishwashers in haphazard fashion; trouble ensues when these two types try to live under one roof.

—Jonathan Eig, writing in the *Wall Street Journal*

There are two kinds of people in the world: those who love good food no matter how much it costs and those who would no more spend over sixty dollars a person for a meal than they would run naked through a crowded intersection.

—Elizabeth Evans, writing in the *Orange County Register*

Animal Instincts

There are two kinds of people in this world:

> those who have exotic pets, and those who say, "Look at that attention-starved weirdo walking around with the cockatiel on his shoulder! What's his deal?"
>
> —Film critic Richard Roeper

There are but two kinds of people:

> the righteous who love dogs and the unrighteous who don't.
>
> —Martin Dykman, writing in the St. Petersburg Times

There are two kinds of people in this world:

> cat people and dog people. Actually, there's a third kind: people who think cats are the devil.
>
> —MARK PATINKIN, WRITING IN THE *PROVIDENCE JOURNAL-BULLETIN*

I've always thought there were two kinds of people:

> those who view pets as property, and those who view them as much more than that.
>
> —CELESTE GARRETT, WRITING IN THE *CHICAGO SUN-TIMES*

There are two kinds of people:

> there are people who look like their pets and there are people who wish they did.
>
> —DIANE WHITE, WRITING IN THE *BOSTON GLOBE*

There are two kinds of people in the world. There are those who awaken with a smile to hear the mockingbird singing outside their window. There are others who would like to grab a gun and shoot the damn noisy bird.

—BILL EDMONDS, WRITING IN THE *ST. PETERSBURG TIMES*

For Love of the Game

There are two kinds of people who bring out the best emotions.

> A hero, someone who has done heroic things, and people who have made mistakes. We like to see people get off the ground. That's a little bit of what sports is about.
>
> —DALLAS COWBOYS OWNER JERRY JONES

There are two kinds of people in the world.

> There are people who derive some sort of spiritual regeneration by spending several hours plowing through the *Baseball Encyclopedia*, and there are people who are not in need of psychiatric help.
>
> —BOB RYAN, WRITING IN THE *HOUSTON CHRONICLE*

There are two kinds of people:

> there are people who think the Red Sox have a shot at the World Series and there are people who have finally grown up.
>
> —DIANE WHITE, WRITING IN THE *BOSTON GLOBE*

We used to say there were two kinds of people,

> those who watched wrestling on television and those who watched but didn't admit it.
>
> —LATE CHICAGO CUBS (AND PRO WRESTLING) ANNOUNCER JACK BRICKHOUSE

There are two kinds of people in this world:
> people who make things happen and people who talk about those who make things happen.
>
> —Pro football and baseball great Deion Sanders

There are two kinds of people:
> those who ask and those who go out and get. I went out and got.
>
> —Boxer Nigel Benn

The way I figure it, there are two kinds of people in the world.
> About 98 percent are in one category. They sit along the sidelines and watch the fox hunt. They applaud whoever catches the fox and

then they either boo or knock those who fail to catch the fox. Now, I'm in the 2 percent. I don't always catch the fox and when I don't, I hear about it. But God, I'd always rather go to the hunt than just observe it and talk about it or write about it.

—SINGER NAT KING COLE

The Shopping Call

There are two kinds of people you cannot buy presents for:

> One is men, the other is husbands. If your husband is a man, the situation is utterly impossible. . . . Make no mistake—the issue is manliness. Anything chosen by a woman is potentially sissy.
>
> —SYNDICATED COLUMNIST ALICE KAHN

There are two kinds of mothers in this world:

> those who are easy to buy presents for (they enthusiastically wear whatever their little angels give them) and those with very, very crowded attics.
>
> —FROM *GOOD HOUSEKEEPING*

There are two kinds of people in the world: those who brake for yard sales, and those who wouldn't stop if the Hope diamond had just been tossed onto the dollar table.

—JENNA RUSSELL, WRITING IN THE BANGOR, MAINE, *DAILY NEWS*

There are two kinds of people: the ones who love to shop and the ones, like me, who would rather have their hair pulled out.

—PARALEGAL AND FRUSTRATED ONLINE SHOPPER EILEEN HAAS-LINDE, QUOTED IN THE *CHICAGO TRIBUNE*

There are two kinds of people in the world: people who love to shop at outlets, and people who would rather drag their nails across a chalkboard.

—TOM LONGSHAW, WRITING IN THE ROCK HILL, SOUTH CAROLINA, *HERALD*

IT TAKES TWO

There are two kinds of people in the world: those who collect things and those who throw things away.

—PEPSI SOUVENIR COLLECTOR BOB STODDARD, QUOTED IN THE *LOS ANGELES TIMES*

There are two kinds of people in the malls on the day after Thanksgiving: those who love to be there and those who would rather be home eating leftover turkey.

—PHYLLIS GILLESPIE, WRITING IN THE *ARIZONA REPUBLIC*

When it comes to catalogues, there are two kinds of people. Some greet the catalogues overflowing the mailbox at [the holidays] with glee. Their idea of a good time is to stretch out on the sofa and peruse the glossy photographs of merchandise that's just a phone call or postage stamp away. The other kind hates catalogues. For these people, the glee comes from throwing the daily offerings in the trash. They may have had an unpleasant experience, or they may simply prefer the challenge of seeking bargains in stores, where they can try on clothes and otherwise examine the real thing.

—Terri Shaw, writing in the *Washington Post*

There are two kinds of people in the world: there are those who, when buying [gas], always know what the number of their pump is when asked by the cashier, and those to whom it has never occurred to look, even though this is the thousandth time they have been asked.

—Miles Kington, writing in the *London Independent*

There are two kinds of people in the world.

One kind wouldn't even consider someone else's old clothes. (Don't they smell? Don't you wonder if the person who wore them is dead?) And then there are those who live for the thrill of the hunt.

—Jenna Russell, writing in the Bangor, Maine, *Daily News*

THE SHOPPING CALL

There are people who buy things because of advertising
> and there are people who buy things in spite of it.
>
> —DIANE WHITE, WRITING IN THE *BOSTON GLOBE*

There are two kinds of people who don't pay for things—
> cops and crooks.
>
> —RICHARD COHEN, WRITING IN THE *WASHINGTON POST*

Home Suite Home

There are two kinds of people in this world. The first attacks a home-improvement project with a Black & Decker. The second does it with a credit card.

—Karen Sandstrom, writing in the *Portland Oregonian*

There are two kinds of people. There are those who hear the phrase "home improvement" and immediately reach for the drill, the hammer, and the utility knife. And then there are the rest of us whose first impulse is to reach for the Yellow Pages.

—Michael E. Kanell, writing in the *Atlanta Journal-Constitution*

There are two kinds of people in the world: people who call the plumber and people who fix the toilet.

—BOOKS THAT WORK PRESIDENT DAN LEVIN

There are two kinds of people in this world: serious-minded souls who read instruction manuals cover-to-cover before they undertake a project, and those folk who are born tinkerers.

—PATRIZIA DILUCCHIO, WRITING IN *WHOLE EARTH NEWS*

There are two kinds of people in this world: those who make careful measurements before they hang a picture and those who just drive a nail into the wall. The first kind always marries the second kind.

—SYNDICATED COLUMNIST ROGER SIMON

I've learned there are two kinds of people: those who turn off a light when they leave a room and those who don't.... "Why don't you just turn on EVERY light in the house?" my husband says glibly upon arriving home from work to our illuminated casa.

—KATHRYN LEIBOVICH, WRITING IN THE RIVERSIDE, CALIFORNIA, *PRESS-ENTERPRISE*

In our neighborhood, and probably in yours, there are two kinds of people. Those who obsess over every claw of crabgrass and every dandelion dagger, and those who believe in equal opportunity for anything remotely green.

—BETH MACY, WRITING IN THE ROANOKE, VIRGINIA, *TIMES & WORLD NEWS*

Pool owners say there are two kinds of people:

> those who want a pool, and those who have one but wish they didn't.
>
> —MAILE CARPENTER, WRITING IN THE *ARIZONA REPUBLIC*

America is divided into two kinds of people:

> those who hate mobile homes and the 10 million who live in them.
>
> —HENRY ALLEN, WRITING IN THE *WASHINGTON POST*

Driving Pursuits

There are two kinds of people in the world: fireside people and travelers. Always one wishes to be a bit of the other.

—Actress Fiona Shaw

Frontiers traditionally attract two kinds of people: the enterprising and energetic, and those escaping from somewhere else.

—Robert Lindsey, writing in the *New York Times*

There are two kinds of people. There are those who go into a cave, see a dark passage, and say, "Let's get out of here." And there are those who wonder what's around the corner.

—Spelunker John Scheltens, quoted in the *New York Times*

There are two kinds of people:

> those who want to get to the airport two hours before flight time and those who think they're wasting their lives if they don't leap on board as the door is closing.
>
> —Syndicated columnist Richard Reeves

It has been said that there are two kinds of people in the world:

> those who love city life and those who don't. Some people are energized by the hustle and bustle, while others prefer quiet and greenery. Of course, we all need both kinds of experience.
>
> —Ted Wilcox, writing in the *Toronto Star*

IT TAKES TWO

There are two kinds of people:
> there are people who brake for yellow lights and there are people who accelerate.
>
> —DIANE WHITE, WRITING IN THE *BOSTON GLOBE*

There are two kinds of pedestrians:
> the quick and the dead.
>
> —UNKNOWN

There are two kinds of people in the world.
> There are those who need to put on the brakes and those who need to step on the gas.
>
> —CHERYL LAVIN, WRITING IN THE *CHICAGO TRIBUNE*

There are two kinds of people in this world:
> those who love valet parking and those who consider it a giant pain in

the neck. Count me among the latter.
Valet parking is the only service I
know of where you pay perfect
strangers to disappear with one of
your most expensive possessions.

—JOHN GROGAN, WRITING IN THE FT. LAUDERDALE
SUN-SENTINEL

Handicapped parking spaces are occupied by two kinds of people:

    1. Handicapped people.

    2. Insensitive jerks in a hurry.

—BILL HALL, WRITING IN THE LEWISTON, IDAHO,
MORNING TRIBUNE

There are two kinds of people:

those who lock their cars and get
them stolen, and those who leave the

keys in the ignition regularly and have never experienced a car theft.

—Tony Chamberlain, writing in the *Boston Globe*

It turns out there are two kinds of people: people who own trucks and people who want to borrow them.

—Paul Turner, writing in the *Spokane Spokesman-Review*

There are two kinds of people on this earth: those who like cutesy personal license plates and those who think they cause traffic accidents because people begin hurling when they spot them.

—*Orlando Sentinel* columnist "Commander Coconut"

There are two kinds of people:

> there are people who have car phones and there are people who drive with at least one hand on the wheel.
>
> —DIANE WHITE, WRITING IN THE *BOSTON GLOBE*

When it comes to packing for trips, there are two kinds of people:

> those who travel light and those who hardly venture out the door without traveler's checks, pre-stamped postcards, dental floss, and a change of underwear. Often, we end up married to each other.
>
> —CHRIS VERNER, WRITING IN THE *ATLANTA JOURNAL-CONSTITUTION*

IT TAKES TWO

There are two kinds of people in the world, and I am one of them.

I'm the kind of person who likes to be on time for things. In fact, I like to be early. Let's say I need to catch a flight that's leaving at 4 P.M. In planning my drive to the airport, I'll factor in a "cushion" to allow for the unexpected, such as heavy traffic, or a flat tire, or being kidnapped. Usually I'm at the gate, ticket out, ready to go, no later than 7:14 A.M. My wife is the other kind of person. For her, the ideal way to catch a plane would be to arrive at the airport as the plane was taking off. She'd stand at the end of the runway, and as the plane flew over her, it would snatch her up with a big hook. Even then, she'd wait until the last second. "What's the hurry?" she'd say. "The plane isn't even halfway down the runway yet!"

—Humorist Dave Barry